Gi

by Iain Gray

LangSyne
PUBLISHING
WRITING *to* REMEMBER

LangSyne
PUBLISHING
WRITING *to* REMEMBER

79 Main Street, Newtongrange,
Midlothian EH22 4NA
Tel: 0131 344 0414 Fax: 0845 075 6085
E-mail: info@lang-syne.co.uk
www.langsyneshop.co.uk

Design by Dorothy Meikle
Printed by Printwell Ltd

ISBN 978-1-85217-759-1

Gilmore

MOTTO:
Pabbay family
(Morrison)

CREST:
A hand clutching a dagger, arising from a castellated tower

TERRITORIES:
Lewis, Harris, North Uist

NAME variations include:
Gillmor
Gillmore
Gilmour

Chapter one:

The origins of the clan system

by Rennie McOwan

The original Scottish clans of the Highlands and the great families of the Lowlands and Borders were gatherings of families, relatives, allies and neighbours for mutual protection against rivals or invaders.

Scotland experienced invasion from the Vikings, the Romans and English armies from the south. The Norman invasion of what is now England also had an influence on land-holding in Scotland. Some of these invaders stayed on and in time became 'Scottish'.

The word clan derives from the Gaelic language term 'clann', meaning children, and it was first used many centuries ago as communities were formed around tribal lands in glens and mountain fastnesses.

The format of clans changed over the centuries, but at its best the chief and his family held the land on behalf of all, like trustees, and the ordinary clansmen and women believed they had a blood relationship with the founder of their clan.

There were two way duties and obligations. An inadequate chief could be deposed and replaced by someone of greater ability.

Clan people had an immense pride in race. Their relationship with the chief was like adult children to a father and they had a real dignity.

The concept of clanship is very old and a more feudal notion of authority gradually crept in.

Pictland, for instance, was divided into seven principalities ruled by feudal leaders who were the strongest and most charismatic leaders of their particular groups.

By the sixth century the 'British' kingdoms of Strathclyde, Lothian and Celtic Dalriada (Argyll) had emerged and Scotland, as one nation, began to take shape in the time of King Kenneth MacAlpin.

Some chiefs claimed descent from ancient kings which may not have been accurate in every case.

By the twelfth and thirteenth centuries the clans and families were more strongly brought under the central control of Scottish monarchs.

Lands were awarded and administered more and more under royal favour, yet the power of the area clan chiefs was still very great.

The long wars to ensure Scotland's

independence against the expansionist ideas of English monarchs extended the influence of some clans and reduced the lands of others.

Those who supported Scotland's greatest king, Robert the Bruce, were awarded the territories of the families who had opposed his claim to the Scottish throne.

In the Scottish Borders country – the notorious Debatable Lands – the great families built up a ferocious reputation for providing warlike men accustomed to raiding into England and occasionally fighting one another.

Chiefs had the power to dispense justice and to confiscate lands and clan warfare produced a society where martial virtues – courage, hardiness, tenacity – were greatly admired.

Gradually the relationship between the clans and the Crown became strained as Scottish monarchs became more orientated to life in the Lowlands and, on occasion, towards England.

The Highland clans spoke a different language, Gaelic, whereas the language of Lowland Scotland and the court was Scots and in more modern times, English.

Highlanders dressed differently, had different

customs, and their wild mountain land sometimes seemed almost foreign to people living in the Lowlands.

It must be emphasised that Gaelic culture was very rich and story-telling, poetry, piping, the clarsach (harp) and other music all flourished and were greatly respected.

Highland culture was different from other parts of Scotland but it was not inferior or less sophisticated.

Central Government, whether in London or Edinburgh, sometimes saw the Gaelic clans as a challenge to their authority and some sent expeditions into the Highlands and west to crush the power of the Lords of the Isles.

Nevertheless, when the eighteenth century Jacobite Risings came along the cause of the Stuarts was mainly supported by Highland clans.

The word Jacobite comes from the Latin for James – Jacobus. The Jacobites wanted to restore the exiled Stuarts to the throne of Britain.

The monarchies of Scotland and England became one in 1603 when King James VI of Scotland (1st of England) gained the English throne after Queen Elizabeth died.

The Union of Parliaments of Scotland and England, the Treaty of Union, took place in 1707.

Some Highland clans, of course, and Lowland families opposed the Jacobites and supported the incoming Hanoverians.

After the Jacobite cause finally went down at Culloden in 1746 a kind of ethnic cleansing took place. The power of the chiefs was curtailed. Tartan and the pipes were banned in law.

Many emigrated, some because they wanted to, some because they were evicted by force. In addition, many Highlanders left for the cities of the south to seek work.

Many of the clan lands became home to sheep and deer shooting estates.

But the warlike traditions of the clans and the great Lowland and Border families lived on, with their descendants fighting bravely for freedom in two world wars.

Remember the men from whence you came, says the Gaelic proverb, and to that could be added the role of many heroic women.

The spirit of the clan, of having roots, whether Highland or Lowland, means much to thousands of people.

Meanwhile, many families proudly boast the heraldic device known as a Coat of Arms, as featured on our front cover.

The central motif of the Coat of Arms would originally have been what was sometimes borne on the shield of a warrior to distinguish himself from others on the battlefield.

Not featured on the Coat of Arms, but highlighted on page three, is the family motto and related crest – with the latter frequently different from the central motif.

Clan warfare produced a society where courage and tenacity were greatly admired

Chapter two:

Letters of fire and sword

A name with a number of points of origin, 'Gilmore' and its spelling variants that include 'Gillmor', 'Gillmore' and 'Gilmour' has both Scottish Gaelic and Irish Gaelic roots.

In the form in which it was known in the Highlands, it derives from *Mac Gille Mhoire*, and in Ireland from *Mac Giolla Mhuire* – both denoting 'son of the servant', or 'devotee of the (Virgin) Mary'.

Another Scottish source is from the Gaelic *Gill-mohr*, meaning 'great servant' and which was bestowed on armour bearers to clan chiefs, while the Irish *Mac Giolla Mhir* denotes 'son of the spirited lad.'

Whatever the origins of the name in the dim and distant past, what is known with certainty is that from earliest times the Gilmores were regarded as a sept, or sub-branch, of Clan Morrison.

Derived from the Gaelic *clanna*, meaning 'children', a clan was a close-knit tribal grouping settled in a particular territory and whose members – or 'children', or 'kin' – owed unswerving loyalty to a chief who, in turn, was bound by duty and honour to protect them.

Not all members of a clan, such as the Gilmores, necessarily shared the same surname as the chief – known as *ceann-cinnidh*, meaning 'head and chief of the family' – and these 'kindred of the clan', or 'kinsfolk', were recognised, as they are to this day, as septs, or sub-branches of the clan.

As such, they are entitled to share in the clan's heritage and traditions that include the right to display its tartan and heraldry of crest and motto – this heraldry recognised by the Lord Lyon King of Arms of Scotland, the final arbiter on all matters heraldic.

In the case of the Gilmores/Morrisons, the proud motto is 'Pabbay family', denoting one of the clan's territorial holdings on Harris, while the crest is a hand clutching a dagger, arising from a castellated tower.

Over the centuries, the fate of the Gilmores was so inextricably linked with that of the Morrisons that they effectively share the same history of both glorious fortune and tragic misfortune.

The Morrisons are thought to have sprung from three very different origins, with the chieftainship of the clan recognised today as lying with the

Morrisons of Ruchdi, on North Uist, who trace a descent back to the Morrisons of Lewis.

But who were these original Morrisons of Lewis? There are two quite separate traditions.

One is that a son of a Norwegian king was shipwrecked at sea and managed to survive the freezing waters of the Outer Hebrides by clinging for dear life to a piece of driftwood.

He was washed up on the shores of Lewis, where he settled, known under the Gaelic name of *Ghille Mhuire* – 'Servant of (the Virgin) Mary'.

Also known as the 'Devotees of Mary', the clan of Ghille Mhuire were later known under the anglicised form of 'Morrison', or 'Morison', and claim a Scandinavian descent from their original shipwrecked ancestor.

The Morrisons also claim a descent from a family of O'Muirgheasains, from Inshowen, in County Donegal, Ireland, who settled on Lewis at an undetermined date.

Morrisons claiming a descent from the Hebridean Morrisons also found a home on the northwest mainland of Scotland, while an unrelated family of Morrisons, known as 'the sons of Maurice' held territory in Perthshire and Aberdeenshire.

The genealogy of the Hebridean Morrisons is understandably tangled when we realise that the original O'Muirgheasains and the original clan of Ghille Mhuire intermarried.

Their history, and by association that of the Gilmores, is also intertwined with neighbouring clans such as Clan Donald, the Macleods, the MacAulays, the Gows and the Mackenzies.

It was under the Macleods that the Morrisons and their septs held Habost, in the north of Lewis, and the ancient hereditary office of *brilheanh* – the honoured position of brieve, or 'one who sits in judgement', and is known to have been held by the Morrisons by at least the late 13th century.

The first recorded Anglicised form of 'Morrison' occurs in the 16th century, in relation to Uisdean (Hugh) the Brieve, a contemporary of Roderick Macleod, chief of the Macleods of Lewis from 1532 until 1595.

Hugh is said to have treacherously betrayed Torquil Dubh Macleod to the rival Mackenzies, who beheaded him in 1597.

A descendant of those Morrisons whose ancestor was the son of a Norwegian king settled at Pabbay, in Harris, where they became noted smiths and armourers.

The Morrisons of Ruchdi, on North Uist, are descendants of these Pabbay Morrisons, and that is why the chieftainship of the clan is invested in them and why 'Pabbay family' is the clan and the Gilmore motto.

The power of the Morrisons increased in 1346 when Cedhain, a relation of the mighty MacDonald Lords of the Isles, married the heiress of a Morrison of Lewis.

But the succeeding centuries saw their power

and influence dramatically wane, as not only rival clans but the power of the mainland monarch brought internecine and bloody warfare to the Hebrides.

During the reign of James VI, an Act of Parliament was passed in 1597 to suppress what was considered to be the 'barbarous inhumanity' of Highlanders and Islanders such as the Morrisons and their Gilmore kinsfolk.

The monarch, certainly no friend of his far flung western seaboard and northern subjects, accordingly issued what were known as *Letters of Fire and Sword* to bring the unruly clansmen to heel.

In what became known as the Daunting of the Isles, Lewis was signalled out for special attention in a campaign that would today be described as a form of ethnic cleansing.

Seeking to justify the savage attack to be launched on the islanders, the Privy Council condemned 'the beastly and monstrous cruelties' that they inflicted upon one another, and pointed out that the rich and fertile lands of Lewis would be better managed by others.

Accordingly, in 1598, the king issued a charter, or contract, to a band of speculators who became known as the Fife Adventurers.

Backed by a 600-strong force of mercenaries led by the Duke of Lennox, the adventurers attempted to wipe out the inhabitants of Lewis and take their lands for themselves.

They received a rude shock, however, when a hardy band of natives fought back with such ferocity that the adventurers were forced to withdraw; another force was later sent to renew the attempt at bringing the clansmen to heel, but this also proved abortive.

Meanwhile, Mackenzie of Kintail had offered his support to the Privy Council because he wished to take advantage of the downfall of the rival Macleods, and through the confused loyalties of the time, the Morrisons had sided with the Mackenzies.

When Mackenzie of Kintail eventually succeeded in buying up the charters the king had granted to the adventurers and imposed his control on Lewis, however, the only reward the Morrisons and their kinsfolk received for their support was to be driven from their lands.

A number of Morrison families such as the Gilmores fled Lewis and eventually settled in the Mackay lands near Durness, in Sutherland, while other Morrisons and their kinsfolk found refuge with the Macleans of Duart, on Mull.

Further desperate attempts were made to stamp the authority of the Crown on the Highlands and Islands through the Statutes of Iona of 1609 and parallel legislation in 1616.

The Morrisons and their kinsfolk such as the Gilmores were among the many who suffered from this attempt to impose Lowland standards on their ancient way of life.

Bards were to be treated in the same manner as beggars, and likely to have their ears cut off and banished – facing death by hanging if they returned – while attempts were also made to replace the Gaelic language with English and the translation of the Bible into Gaelic was banned.

Strict controls were also enforced on the distilling of whisky to prevent its illegal sale, with ordinary folk allowed to distil whisky, but only in their own homes and for their own use.

This ended badly for the Morrisons of Pabbay and their Gilmore kinsfolk – at some stage in the early 17th century they are believed to have been forced off their lands for illegally distilling this cherished 'usquebagh', the 'water of life.'

Chapter three:

Fame and infamy

Bearers of the Gilmore name and its popular spelling variants have achieved high political office and distinction in the cut-throat world of politics – while others of the name have gained infamy through decidedly more murderous pursuits.

Born in London in 1926, Sir Ian Gilmour, more formally known as Baron Gilmour of Craigmillar, was the leading British Conservative Party politician whose views were frequently out of step with mainstream conservative thought.

Elected MP (Member of Parliament) for Central Norfolk in 1962 and later, from 1974 until his retirement in 1992, for Chesham and Amersham, he held a number of senior government posts including Secretary of State for Defence under Prime Minister Edward Heath and, under Prime Minister Margaret Thatcher, Lord Privy Seal from 1979 to 1981.

From an aristocratic background, he was the son of the wealthy stockbroker Lieutenant Colonel Sir John Gilmour, 2nd Baronet, and Victoria, a granddaughter of the 5th Earl of Cadogan.

A social liberal, he favoured the legalisation of abortion and homosexuality and the abolition of the death penalty.

A supporter of the campaign to join what was then the European Economic Community (EEC), he was also opposed to the Commonwealth Immigration Act of 1968, decrying it as racist while, along with then Defence Secretary Lord Carrington, in 1979 he chaired the Lancaster House talks which led to the end of Ian Smith's government in Rhodesia and the creation of Zimbabwe.

Married to Lady Caroline Margaret Montagu-Douglas-Scott, daughter of the 8th Duke of Buccleuch and formally styled Sir Ian Gilmour, 3rd Baronet and elevated to the peerage in 1992 as Baron Gilmour of Craigmillar, of Craigmillar in the District of Edinburgh – with which his family had maintained a close relationship for hundreds of years – he died in 2007.

He is portrayed by the actor Pip Torrens in the 2011 biographical film of Margaret Thatcher, *The Iron Lady*, while he was the father of the historian and biographer Sir David Gilmour, 4th Baronet, born in 1952, and the classical music conductor Oliver Gilmour, born in 1953.

With the spelling variant 'Gillmore', David

Gillmore, elevated to the peerage in 1996 as Baron Gillmore of Thamesfield, of Putney in the London Borough of Wandsworth, was the distinguished British diplomat born in 1934.

Joining the Foreign and Commonwealth Office in 1970, posts he held before his death in 1999 include First Secretary (Commercial) Moscow and head of the Defence Department, Foreign and Commonwealth Office.

One particularly infamous bearer of the Gilmore name and one whose ultimate fate had a particular resonance at the time – and the subject of books, film and song – was the American murderer Gary Gilmore.

What brought him to attention was not only the murders he committed, but that in 1977 he became the first person to be executed in the United States in ten years, dismissed all attempts to have his sentence commuted and demanded it be carried out by firing squad.

Born into a dysfunctional family in McCamey, Texas, in 1940, his father Frank Gilmore was an alcoholic and confidence trickster who had married Bessie (née) Brown in Provo, Utah in 1913.

Frequently on the move and making a living

by selling fake magazine subscriptions and adopting the surname 'Coffman' in an attempt to evade the law, his son was actually christened Faye Robert Coffman.

Once the family left Texas, for Portland, Oregon, his mother changed his name to Gary Mark Gilmore.

Dropping out of high school in his ninth grade – although scoring 133 in his IQ test and displaying aptitude and artistic skills, he began a life of crime when aged 14 by operating a small ring of car thieves with friends.

Arrested but released with a warning, he was arrested again only two weeks later for car theft and sent to reform school for a year.

His criminal activities escalated as he displayed much wilder tendencies, frequently alcohol-fuelled and, in 1964, he was sentenced to 15 years imprisonment in the Oregon State Penitentiary for assault and armed robbery.

Diagnosed by a prison psychiatrist as having an anti-social personality disorder and 'intermittent psychotic decompensation', he was nevertheless granted conditional release in 1972 to live at weekends in a half-way house run by the authorities and attend art studies.

But it took only a month for his violent tendencies to resurface and, arrested and convicted of armed robbery, he was incarcerated in the maximum security facility of the federal prison in Marion, Illinois.

Conditionally paroled in April of 1975, he went to live with a distant cousin, Brenda Nicol, in Provo, Utah and obtained a job in an uncle's cobblers' business and, later, with an insulation company.

But he again reverted to his destructive lifestyle of drinking, stealing and fighting.

Matters came to a violent and tragic head on July 19, 1976 when he robbed and murdered Max Jensen, a young gas station attendant, in Orem, Utah.

Only one night later, he also murdered Bennie Bushnell, a motel manager in Orem and who, in common with the first victim, was a student at Brigham Young University and married with young children.

Both men, chillingly, had been killed in the same callous manner – complying with his demand to lie down and then shot in the head with a .22 calibre pistol.

The bloody evidence trail eventually led to Gilmore and he was arrested and charged with the murder of both men – although because of complex legal issues the Jensen case was never brought to trial.

Charged with the murder of Bushnell, his trial began at Provo Courthouse on October 5, 1976 and, lasting only two days, the jury unanimously found him guilty and recommended the death penalty.

This came at a landmark period in the American justice system, because the U.S. Supreme Court had just upheld a new series of death penalty statutes – overturning a ruling based on another murder trial, that all states should commute death sentences to life imprisonment.

Despite his opposition to the moves, the American Civil Liberties Union (ACLU) and others attempted to have the death sentence commuted, but to no avail.

From death row Gilmore, set to be the first person in ten years to be executed in the United States, declared: "They always want to get in on the act. I don't think they have ever really done anything effective in their lives.

"I would like them all – including that group of reverends and rabbis from Salt Lake City – to butt out.

"This is my life and this is my death. It's been sanctioned by the courts that I die, and I accept that."

At the time, Utah had two methods of

execution – by hanging or by firing squad – and Gilmore chose the latter.

Accordingly, on January 17, 1977, at Utah State Prison in Draper, Utah, he was executed by a four-strong firing squad – three loaded with live ammunition and one with blanks, so that none could be certain who fired the fatal shots.

Having requested that his organs be donated for transplant, two people received his corneas – later the macabre subject of *Gary Gilmore's Eyes*, a song by the punk rock band The Adverts – and the book *The Executioner's Song*, by Norman Mailer and winner of the 1980 Pulitzer Prize and, based on the book, the 1982 film of the name with Tommy Lee Jones as Gilmore.

Pursuing a much more peaceful path in life, Gilmore's younger brother Mikal Gilmore, born in Portland, Oregon in 1951, is the music journalist and writer whose 1994 memoir *Shot in the Heart* chronicles his troubled relationship with his brother and the rest of his family.

Chapter four:

On the world stage

Along with popular spelling variants that include Gillmor and Gilmour, bearers of the Gilmore name have achieved international fame and acclaim through a colourful range of endeavours and pursuits.

With the spelling variant 'Gilmour', **Dave Gilmour**, born in Cambridge in 1946, is the guitarist and vocalist of the progressive rock band Pink Floyd.

Joining the band in 1968 following the departure of founding member Syd Barrett, he has enjoyed success with iconic albums that include the 1973 *The Dark Side of the Moon*, the 1975 *Wish You Were Here* and, from 1979, *The Wall*.

Remaining with the band following the departure of bassist, vocalist and fellow songwriter Roger Waters in 1985 and releasing more albums in addition to pursuing a solo recording career, he is also credited with having nurtured a young Kate Bush to help her on the road to her own recording success with singles including *Wuthering Heights*.

Ranked by *Rolling Stone* magazine at No. 14

in its list of the greatest guitarists of all time and, as a member of Pink Floyd, an inductee of the UK Music Hall of Fame and the U.S. Rock and Roll Hall of Fame, he was made a CBE in 2003 for his contribution to music.

From progressive rock to jazz, **David Gilmore**, born in 1964 in Cambridge, Massachusetts is the guitarist who has played with bands including M-Base Collective and the jazz fusion outfit Lost Tribe.

Also in the jazz genre, **John Gilmore**, born in Chicago in 1931 and who died in 1995, was the avant-garde saxophonist best known for his collaboration from the 1950s to the 1990s with the keyboardist and bandleader Sun Ra.

From jazz to country music, **Jimmie Dale Gilmore** is the American singer, songwriter and producer born in 1945 in Amarillo, Texas who, along with his band The Flatlanders has recorded albums including the 2002 *Now Again*.

In an earlier century and much different musical genre, **Patrick Sarsfield Gilmore** was the Irish-American bandmaster and composer born in 1829 in Ballygar, Co. Galway and who died in 1892.

Immigrating to the United States, it was

while serving in the Union Army during the American Civil War of 1861 to 1865 that, in 1863 and under the pseudonym 'Louis Lambert', he wrote the lyrics for *When Johnny Comes Marching Home*.

On the stage, Sherman Virginia Poole was the American stage, film and television actress better known as **Virginia Gilmore**.

Born in 1919 in El Monte, California and married for a time to fellow screen star Yul Brynner, her film credits include *Western Union*, directed by Fritz Lang, and *Swamp Water*, both from 1941; she died in 1986.

On British shores, **Peter Gilmore** was the actor best known for his portrayal from 1971 to 1980 of Captain James Onedin in the popular BBC period drama *The Onedin Line*.

Born in 1931 in Leipzig, Germany, but raised in Yorkshire, his big screen credits include a number of the *Carry On* comedies, the 1966 *The Great St Trinian's Train Robbery*, the 1969 *Oh! What a Lovely War* and, from 1978, *Warlords of Atlantis*, while he also appeared in a number of stage productions including *Lock Up Your Daughters*.

Married for a time to the actress Una Stubbs, he died in 2013.

Back on American shores, **Alexei Gilmore**, born in Manhattan in 1976, is the actress whose television credits include *CSI:Cyber* and among big screen credits are the 2008 *Surfer, Dude* and the 2013 *Willow Creek*.

With his distinctive voice instantly recognisable to American radio and television audiences, Arthur Wells Gilmore, better known as **Art Gilmore**, was born in 1912 in Tacoma, Washington.

Beginning his career as a staff announcer for the Warner Brothers' Hollywood radio station KFWB and then as a news reader for CBS station KNX, and having served during the Second World War as an officer aboard an aircraft carrier, he went on to narrate a number of television shows including *The Red Skelton Show*, *Highway Patrol*, *Dragnet* and *The Waltons*.

A co-founder in 1966 of Pacific Pioneer Broadcasters – which annually presents Art Gilmore Achievement Awards for notable contributions to broadcasting and related industries – and having served from 1961 to 1963 as president of the American Federation of Television and Film Artists, he died in 2010.

Known for his role of Dale Volker in the

television science fiction series *Stargate Universe*, **Patrick Gilmore**, born in 1976 in Edmonton, Alberta, is the son of Canadian retired professional ice hockey forward **Tom Gilmore**.

Born in 1948 in Flin Flon, Manitoba and a star player in a career that included playing 202 games in the World Hockey Association with the Edmonton Oilers and Los Angeles Sharks, Tom Gilmore is also the father of the diplomat and social entrepreneur **Scott Gilmour**, founder of the non-profit organisation Building Markets.

In cycling, **Graeme Gilmour** is the Australian retired track cyclist who was aged only 10 when he started racing.

Born in 1945 in Launceston, Tasmania, winner of the Australian national road race title in 1967 and an inaugural member of the Tasmanian Sporting Hall of Fame, he is the father of the Belgian-Australian retired track cyclist **Matthew Gilmore**.

Born in 1972 in Ghent, Belgium and winner in 1972 along with Etienne De Wilde of a silver medal in the men's Madison event at the 2000 Sydney Olympics, he is a nephew of the late British professional cyclist Tom Simpson.

Born in 1937 in Haswell, Co. Durham and

the recipient of medals including silver at the 1958 British Empire and Commonwealth Games, Simpson collapsed and died while taking part in the thirteenth stage of the 1967 Tour de France.

From sport to the sciences, **Charles Whitney Gilmore**, born in 1874, was the American palaeontologist who gained renown in the late years of the nineteenth century and early years of the twentieth for his work on vertebrate fossils.

This was during his career with the United States National Museum, now the National Museum of Natural History, when he identified many dinosaurs in North America and Mongolia.

These include Bactrosaurus, Parrosaurus and Styracosaurus, while in 1979, thirty-four years after his death, the dinosaur genus Gilmoreosaurus was named in his honour.

Taking to the heavens, **Alan Gilmore** is the New Zealand astronomer who, along with his wife Pamela K. Kilmartin, has discovered a number of minor planets and other astronomical objects.

Born in 1944 in Greymouth, the asteroid 2537 *Gilmore* is named in his honour, while asteroid 3907 *Kilmartin* is named in honour of his wife.

Bearers of the Gilmore name and its spelling

variant 'Gillmor' have also excelled in the creative world of art.

Born in 1936 in Reading, Berkshire, **Robert Gillmor** is the ornithologist, artist, illustrator and author who co-founded the Society of Wildlife Artists (SWLA) in the early 1960s and a recipient of the RSPB (Royal Society for the Protection of Birds) Medal.

An American water colourist and printmaker, **Ada Gilmore** – also known by her married name Ada Gilmore Chafee – was a founding member in 1951 of thc Provincctown Printers, in Massachusetts.

Born in 1883 in Kalamazoo, Michigan and spending some of her early life living with an aunt in Northern Ireland after being orphaned, she studied at Belfast School of Art; returning to America and studying at the Art Institute of Chicago and having exhibited widely, she died in 1955.

From art to literature, **John 'Jonathan' Gilmore**, born in Los Angeles in 1935, was the American author and friend of the actor James Dean and fellow authors William S. Burroughs and Jack Kerouac known for his true crime works, fiction and Hollywood memoirs.

He died in 2016, the author of books including the 1976 *The Real James Dean*, the 1994

Severed: The True Story of the Black Dahlia Murder and, from 2009, *Hollywood Boulevard*.

One bearer of the Gilmore name with a rather unusual claim to fame was **Joe Gilmore**, who literally shook his way to fame as head barman of the Savoy Hotel's American Bar for a record 21 years.

Born in Belfast in 1922 and moving to London when aged 16, he began working as a trainee barman in the London hotel in 1940.

Appointed head barman of the American Bar in 1955 and holding the position until he retired in 1976, he became cocktail maker to the stars and the inventor of a number of exotic concoctions to celebrate particular people or events.

Celebrities he served over the years include stars of stage and screen Charlie Chaplin, Laurel and Hardy, Grace Kelly, Errol Flynn, Joan Crawford, Frank Sinatra, Ingrid Bergman and Laurence Olivier.

He died in 2015, while among the special cocktails he created and mixed were the *Blenheim*, to mark Sir Winston Churchill's 90th birthday in 1964, the *Missouri Mule* for U.S. President Harry S. Truman and, in 1969, the *Moonwalk* to mark the first moon landing.